Little People, BIG DREAMS

MARIE CURIE

Written by
Mª Isabel Sánchez Vegara

Illustrated by
Frau Isa

Translated by Emma Martinez

Lincoln
Children's Books

When Marie was a little girl, she made a vow to herself . . .
she was going to be a scientist, not a princess.

Marie was from a poor family, but she was very smart.
At school, she won a gold medal for her studies, which
she kept in her drawer like a treasure.

Marie couldn't go to the same university as her brother. In her home country, only men were allowed to study. But she wouldn't take no for an answer, so she packed her bags and moved away to France.

Even though studying in a new language was not easy, Marie soon became the best math and science student in Paris!

One day, Marie met Pierre, and happily . . .
he loved science just like her.

Soon, Pierre and Marie loved each other, too.

They married and became
Madame and Monsieur Curie!

Hidden away in their laboratory, Marie and Pierre discovered two incredible things: radium and polonium.

It was such a thrilling moment for science!

They won a Nobel Prize for their research! Marie became the first woman to receive this honor.

One day, Pierre was in a terrible accident, and
poor Marie was left alone.

Marie wiped her tears away and worked harder than ever. The audience applauded loudly the day she was awarded her second Nobel Prize.

A terrible war broke out. Marie's discoveries were used by doctors to help injured soldiers.

After the war was over, many girls followed in Marie's footsteps, studying at her Parisian institute.

She had valuable advice for every new student: in life, there is nothing to be afraid of, only many things to learn, and many ways to help those in need.

MARIE CURIE

(Born 1867 • Died 1934)

c.1869
(third from left)

1895

Marie Curie was born Maria Salomea Skłodowska in Warsaw,
Poland. She is most famous for winning two Nobel Prizes—one for
Physics and one for Chemistry. She was the first female scientist
to win a Nobel Prize, and the only female, so far, to win two in
different subjects. She was a remarkable child, with an incredible
love of learning. She overcame the loss of her mother at the age of
ten to become a brilliant student. Despite Maria's talent, she wasn't
allowed to go to the same university as her brother because she was
a girl. She worked as a teacher and a governess before moving to
Paris to study—where she became Marie. It was at this time that she

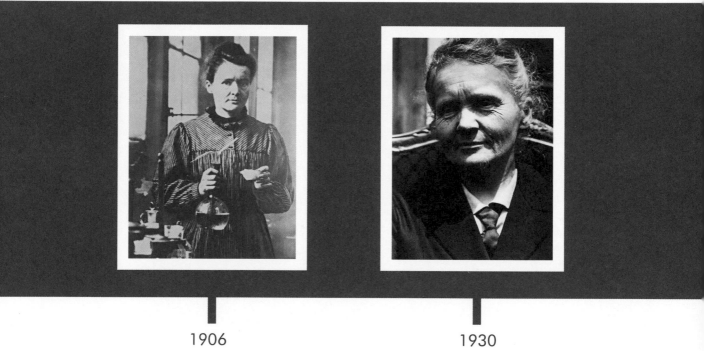

1906   1930

met Pierre Curie. They later married and, together, made the great scientific discovery of polonium and radium, and in 1903, they won the Nobel Prize for Physics. After the sudden loss of Pierre, who was killed in a street accident, Marie threw herself into work. She won a second Nobel Prize—this time for Chemistry—founded the Radium Institute at the University of Paris, and developed the use of X-rays to help injured soldiers in the First World War. Marie believed in the beauty of science, and that people would use science for good, not evil. She used all of her skills to search for knowledge, and her discoveries continue to help people with illnesses today.

Want to find out more about **Marie Curie**?
Have a read of these great books:

Who Was Marie Curie? by Megan Stine and Nancy Harrison
Women in Science: 50 Fearless Pioneers Who Changed the World
by Rachel Ignotofsky
DK Biography: Marie Curie by Vicki Cobb

If you're in Paris, France, you could even visit the office and laboratory
of Marie Curie. Or experience a virtual tour here:
http://musee.curie.fr/visiter/visiteurs-individuels/visite-guidee

Brimming with creative inspiration, how-to projects, and useful
information to enrich your everyday life, Quarto Knows is a favourite
destination for those pursuing their interests and passions. Visit our
site and dig deeper with our books into your area of interest:
Quarto Creates, Quarto Cooks, Quarto Homes, Quarto Lives,
Quarto Drives, Quarto Explores, Quarto Gifts, or Quarto Kids.

First published in the UK in 2017. This gift book and paper doll set published in 2018
by Lincoln Children's Books, an imprint of The Quarto Group.
400 First Avenue North, Suite 400, Minneapolis, MN 55401, USA.
T (612) 344-8100 F (612) 344-8692 **www.QuartoKnows.com**

Text copyright © 2016 by Mª Isabel Sánchez Vegara
Illustrations copyright © 2016 by Frau Isa

First published in Spain in 2016 under the title *Pequeña & Grande Marie Curie*
by Alba Editorial (www.albaeditorial.es)

A catalogue record for this book is available from the British Library.

ISBN 978-1-78603-401-4

Manufactured in Guangdong, China CC052018

1 3 5 7 9 8 6 4 2

Photographic acknowledgements (pages 28-29, from left to right) 1. Marie Curie as a young girl, c. 1869 © Lebrecht Music and
Arts Photo Library, Alamy Stock Photo 2. Marie and Pierre Curie, 1895 © AFP, Getty Images 3. Marie Curie, 1906 © Hulton Archive,
Getty Images 4. Portrait of Marie Curie, 1930 © Ewing Galloway, Alamy Stock Photo

Also in the *Little People,* **BIG DREAMS** series:

FRIDA KAHLO

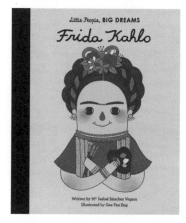

ISBN: 978-1-84780-783-0

Frida Kahlo's horrific childhood accident did not stop her from being one of the best artists of the twentieth century.

COCO CHANEL

ISBN: 978-1-84780-784-7

Coco Chanel was a cabaret singer, hat-maker, seamstress, and one of the most famous fashion designers that has ever lived.

MAYA ANGELOU

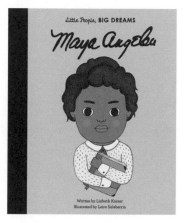

ISBN: 978-1-84780-889-9

After a traumatic event at age eight, Maya Angelou discovered her voice and went on to become one of the world's most beloved writers.

AMELIA EARHART

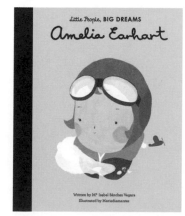

ISBN: 978-1-84780-888-2

Amelia Earhart's strong will, hard work, and self-belief helped her to become the first female aviator to fly solo across the Atlantic.

AGATHA CHRISTIE

ISBN: 978-1-84780-960-5

Agatha Christie's inventive imagination made her the queen of mystery, and the best-selling novelist of all time.